Just a Book

Dear Reader, even if the words of this book speak only to the heart of one person in a thousand, may you be that person.

Marius Potgieter

Published by: BESTME LTD
21 Woodside Close
Woking
Surrey GU21 2DD, UK
Available from Lulu.com and
Amazon Kindle
and as a paperback from
Amazon and other outlets

To view other books by the author
go to:
www.lulu.com/spotlight/bestme
or
At Amazon
type
Marius Potgieter
in the search box

Personal Testimony

www.personal-testimony.com

This picture, which was drawn by
my grandson when he was still very
young, clearly depicts the covering
hand of God, protecting the little
boat on its way to a city.   A
similar picture was on the tract I

received from a crippled old man, to whom I will refer later.

I want to give this testimony because I live by it. I want to share it; like someone entrusted with a great treasure that he does not want to keep to himself. I do so with humility and respect to all.

Though I was brought up in a Christian home, as a young person I did not believe and did not want to have anything to do with the God that people told me about.

I was rebellious and alone and my parents sent me to a boarding school. There I unfortunately met up with the wrong crowd at first. My mother kept on praying for me all the time

One day when I went to the 'bioscope', as we called a cinema then, an old crippled man who was sitting on the steps next to the entrance gave me a piece of paper with a picture on it and words that described 'the way of salvation.' I did not look at it further, but did not throw it away either.

That evening when I went to bed, I took it from my pocket and looked at it. There was a picture of a man in a boat on his way to a beautiful city. The waves around his boat looked threatening, but I thought by myself that he would make it, because there was a big hand over him to protect him

Suddenly it struck me that if I was the man in the boat I would not have the hand of God to protect me, because I did not believe in Him. This, however, challenged me to seek for the Creator God who made a way for us to know Him through his salvation plan.

My parents invited me to church that Sunday to listen to the evangelist Oswald Smith, and that day I accepted Jesus Christ as my Saviour. This nearly sixty years ago and, though I had a rough patch at the beginning, I have never felt sorry about it. This was a turning point in my life and only after this I decided to go to Medical School.

I am far from perfect and have gone through quite a lot of difficulties and stumblings, but I know I am forgiven and cared for on earth and have hope for eternity. The One whose name many use as a swear word, and others want to remove from

Christmas, and many do not want to think or talk about, has become my Saviour.

And, if I hold on to my faith to the end, when I leave here, I am secure!

"For God so loved the world that he gave his one and only Son, that whoever believes in Him shall not perish but have eternal life." (John 3:16)

Eternal life does not start when you die, it starts the moment you receive Christ as your Saviour. You are then adopted and, by the Spirit, become one of the family of God. Life with Jesus is not always easy but never dull. It is more exciting than anything you can imagine... and it never ends! Why not start today and make these words your own?

"The Lord is my shepherd; I shall not want.
[2] He makes me lie down in green pastures.

He leads me beside still waters.

³ He restores my soul.

He leads me in paths of

righteousness

for his name's sake.

⁴ Even though I walk through the

valley of the shadow of death,

I will fear no evil,

for you are with me;

your rod and your staff,

they comfort me.

⁵ You prepare a table before me

in the presence of my enemies;

you anoint my head with oil;

my cup overflows.

[6] Surely goodness and mercy shall

follow me

all the days of my life,

and I shall dwell in the house of

the Lord

forever"

(Psalm 23 ESV)

God is faithful and God is good

Did you know that it is possible to have a personal relationship with someone who is more wonderful in every way than any other being? The One who created everything, offers you this relationship. He is God, the Creator and Ruler of Heaven and Earth. He offers the only hope for the ultimate eradication of evil. He has an immediate and on-going plan to rescue you from the evil that is haunting the world. He also gives his people the best help and back up available.

If you wonder, then why is the world in such a mess? Just read on and you will find the answer.

As you will see later, it is possible to become part of God's Kingdom, and receive the most wonderful heritage as a gift, the greatest of which is everlasting communion with Him.

The weapons of this Kingdom are the words of God, and faith is the shield.

The ultimate motivation of the Kingdom is Agape, the love that is from God, and not hate, a set of rules, or fear "There is no fear in love. But perfect love drives out fear."

"A new command I give you: Love one another. As I have loved you, so you must love one another."

Love is from God, "so we know and rely on the love God has for us. God is love. Whoever lives in love lives in God, and God in them."

"And now these three remain: faith, hope and love. But the greatest of these is love."

The rule of the Kingdom is: "Love the Lord your God with all your heart and with all your soul and with all your strength and with all your mind; and, love your neighbour as yourself."

"Love is something you do."

The Kingdom can never be advanced by any form of physical force or violence "'Not by might nor by power, but by my Spirit,' says the LORD Almighty."

"Do not suppose that I have come to bring peace to the earth. I did not come to bring peace, but a sword." If you take these words of Jesus in context, they mean that it is non-believers, even from their own household that will persecute believers; not the other way around.

About persecution, Jesus said: "Remember what I told you: 'A servant is not greater than his master.' If they persecuted Me, they will persecute you also. If they obeyed My teaching, they will obey yours also."

"I tell you, my friends, do not be afraid of those who kill the body and after that can do no more. But I will show you whom you should fear: Fear Him who, after your body has been killed, has authority to throw you into hell."

"...a time is coming when anyone who kills you will think he is offering service to God. They will do such things because they have not known the Father or Me."

"You have heard that it was said, 'you shall love your neighbour and hate your enemy.' But I say to you, love your enemies and pray for those who persecute you, so that you may be sons of your Father who is in heaven."

"Do not take revenge, my dear friends, but leave room for God's wrath, for it is written: 'It is Mine to avenge; I will repay,' says the Lord."

Our struggle is against Evil, not against people. "For our struggle is not against flesh and blood, but against the rulers, against the authorities, against the powers of this dark world and against the spiritual forces of evil in the heavenly realms."

The Kingdom is an unseen or spiritual Kingdom, but its citizens all over the world express it on earth. It is an everlasting Kingdom, and our King ensures our victory. In God's Kingdom, we walk in the light because "God is light; in Him there is no darkness at all." Our constitution is written down in the Bible. When you register as a citizen of the Kingdom of God your name is written in 'The Book of Life' and no one can erase it.

"The one who overcomes will, like them, be dressed in white. I will never blot out the name of that person from the book of life."

Though at present the Kingdom's existence is unseen by human senses, it is more real than any worldly kingdom. The Holy Spirit represents Christ in and through each true believer. "... that all of them may be one, Father, just as You are in Me and I am in You. May they also be in us so that the world may believe that You have sent Me."

"Christ in you, the hope of glory. "

We know, not only that God loves us, but that He loved us even before we believed, and that He also loves all those who do not acknowledge Him yet.

"But God demonstrates His own love for us in this: While we were still sinners, Christ died for us."

Christ carried on the cross the sin of the entire world, committed Christians are those who embraced the gift of God's salvation plan, and trust in Jesus. The gift is presented to all. "This is good, and pleases God our Saviour, [4] who wants all people to be saved and to come to a knowledge of the truth."

Jesus said "whoever comes to Me I will never drive away."

We have to have faith and trust in our God. "Without faith it is impossible to please God, because anyone who comes to Him must believe that He exists and that He rewards those who earnestly seek Him."

Christians have their proof in history, faith in the present, and hope in the future.

Our prayers are based on the one Jesus taught us: "Our Father in heaven, Hallowed be Your name. Your kingdom come. Your will be done on earth as it is in heaven.

Give us this day our daily bread, and forgive us our debts, as we also have forgiven our debtors. And lead us not into temptation, but deliver us from evil."

There is great power in prayer if done in the Spirit. It helps to release **the strongest force on earth**, which is love empowered by the Holy Spirit; Who is so much stronger than any unholy spirit or earthly love. And the wonderful thing is, we do not have to be strong in ourselves for God to use us to release his power!

The King

Needs not be elected because there is no one like Him.

Needs not be replaced for He is eternal.

Cannot improve because He is perfect; in love, in righteousness, in holiness and in power.

Lives in the unapproachable light where nothing impure may enter.

Is the Creator of heaven, of earth and

all that is in it. You need only look at the macro-cosmos and the micro-cosmos to have to admit that Someone great and wonderful must be behind the design.

The King who is God presents Himself as Father, Son and Holy Spirit. This is a great mystery, how God can be three Persons but One. It can however be compared, for instance, with lawyer, who is also a husband and a father. Because of the oneness of the Godhead, there is no question of polytheism. Right at the beginning of the bible we read "the Spirit of God was hovering over the waters.

And God said, 'Let there be light,' and there was light"

The Father speaks and Jesus is the Word. (Compare John 1:1-3)
"...as He was praying, heaven was opened and the Holy Spirit descended on Him in bodily form like a dove, and a voice came from heaven, "You are My beloved Son, with You I am well-pleased."

"Therefore go and make disciples of all nations, baptising them in the name of the Father and of the Son and of the Holy Spirit,"

We quench our thirst with living water, which we also give freely to others.

"Let anyone who is thirsty come to Me and drink. Whoever believes in Me, as Scripture has said, rivers of living water will flow from within them."

Our food, like that of Jesus, is to do the will of our Father. "'My food,' said Jesus, 'is to do the will of Him who sent me and to finish His work.'"

"Jesus answered, 'It is written: "Man shall not live on bread alone, but on every word that comes from the mouth of God."'"

The Adversary

How you have fallen from heaven,
O star of the morning, son of the dawn!
You have been cut down to the earth,
You who have weakened the nations!
"But you said in your heart,
'I will ascend to heaven;
I will raise my throne above the stars of
God,
And I will sit on the mount of assembly
In the recesses of the north.
'I will ascend above the heights of the
clouds;
I will make myself like the Most High.'
Isaiah 14:12-14

The angels are created beings, and the one in the highest position was Lucifer, who was so high and mighty that he challenged the position of the King, and became Satan, the adversary, the angel of darkness.

He dishonoured the King and was stripped from his position. Because he would contaminate it, he could no longer experience the presence and the blessing of the King, and when he went away from the King's presence a third of the angels followed him. With their support, he set up an opposing kingdom, the kingdom of darkness, in war with the Kingdom of light. He also convinced humankind to side with him.

If we look around us and see what people do to one another, it is clear that there is also a 'designer of evil'. Satan and his 'spiritual troops' are real: they do not mind, however, that people deny their existence, as this means that they can work undercover. They take what is weak in man and make it worse, or pervert what is natural. They encourage him to work out his own righteousness and deny his Maker. Paul said that our battle is not really with flesh and blood, as we may think about human conflict, but with the evil forces that always oppose us if we want to do the right thing.

Satan's kingdom had to be defeated, and God's honour restored. Judicially, Jesus has accomplished this defeat on the cross.

Though he is on the run, Satan tries to oppose the validity of this verdict, but he is at a loss for there is no higher authority than God to turn to. Before the execution of the judgment on him takes place, Satan is trying to exert himself in as many ways possible against God and His Kingdom.

Humankind

Material or visible things stem from the invisible (in Christian context, the Word) and the 'seen', comes from the 'unseen'. This unseen is real and permanent and will at the end outlast the 'seen.' When John speaks of 'the Word' he is speaking of Jesus.

"In the beginning was the Word, and the Word was with God, and the Word was God. He was with God in the beginning. Through Him all things were made; without Him nothing was made that has been made."

Humans are the crown of God's creation.

"So God created mankind in His own image, in the image of God He created them; male and female He created them."

The human body is so amazing. For instance, the fact that you are able to read and understand what you are reading is a miracle. Images are directed through a clear adaptable lens on the front of your eye onto 120 million rods, and millions of cones in the retina and picked up by nerves leading to a specific area of the occipital lobe of the brain where we 'see'. This area is connected to other areas in the brain where these images are integrated and interpreted, together with auditory impulses that comes from the inner ear via the auditory cortex. Isn't that wonderful?

The Bible teaches that our life does not end here on earth, and there are numerous people with near-death experiences who have testified that this is true. We should not live only for our life on earth.

"What good is it for someone to gain the whole world, yet forfeit their soul?"

Our life on earth is part of our eternal life, to continue in heaven or hell. It goes even further if we consider that the Spirit of God can quicken perceived written or spoken words, especially words from the Bible, to become 'alive' and regenerate and nourish the human spirit, so we are able to 'see' and 'hear' spiritually.

Because of this, there are millions of people on earth who are able to experience communication with God.

"God is spirit, and His worshipers must worship in the Spirit and in truth."

Because God has made mankind in His image, He wants them to be true to Him. Only God has full and perfect knowledge, He expects humankind to discern between good and evil, by the light only He can give.

"For with you is the fountain of life; in your light we see light."

This is the basis of universal order.

He speaks to us mostly through the words of the Bible, which is the truest possible human replica of the eternal Word of God. If you have never read it, why not read it once with an open mind? Start, for instance, with the book of John.

Initially the authority to rule the earth was given to man, but he forfeited this authority by listening to Satan, and becoming subject to him. By this, he transferred his God-given authority of the earth to Satan. Not only did he subject the whole human race to misery, but chaos entered the world, with all the calamities to follow. The immediate effect of their disobedience to God, was that humans died a spiritual death, and later also experienced physical death.

However, God gives everyone the opportunity to turn back to God in repentance and obedience, and so regain his position of authority. In doing this he experiences fierce opposition from Satan and his demons.

"Be self-controlled and alert. Your enemy the devil prowls around like a roaring lion looking for someone to devour."

The attack takes different forms, from outright persecution to mental oppression. There is always deception.

"And no wonder, for Satan himself masquerades as an angel of light."

"the devil …was a murderer from the beginning, not holding to the truth, for there is no truth in him. When he lies, he speaks his native language, for he is a liar and the father of lies.

The Rescue

In the sixth month, God sent the angel Gabriel to Nazareth, a town in Galilee, to a virgin pledged to be married to a man named Joseph, a descendant of David. The virgin's name was Mary. The angel went to her and said, "Greetings, you who are highly favoured! The Lord is with you." Mary was greatly troubled at his words and wondered what kind of greeting this might be. But the angel said to her, "Do not be afraid, Mary, you have found favour with God. You will be with child and give birth to a son, and you are to give him the name Jesus. He will be great and will be

**called the Son of the Most High.
Luke 1:26-32**

The coming of Jesus to the world has
been announced on many occasions
by the prophets of the Old Testament.

"Therefore the Lord Himself will
give you a sign. The virgin will
conceive and give birth to a son,
and will call Him Immanuel." "For a
child will be born to us, a son will be
given to us, and the government will
rest on His shoulders. And His
name will be called Wonderful
Counsellor, Mighty God, Eternal
Father, Prince of Peace."

Central to the Christian message is this: Jesus Christ is not just another prophet or messenger, He is God himself who came to the world in human form. He is thus called both; the Son of God and the Son of man. As one of the Godhead, he came to represent the Father. Though He was crucified, He has risen from the dead, went back to heaven from where He will return. All authority in heaven and on earth has been given to Him. He is King, Priest, Prophet, Saviour, Brother, Friend and Servant to all who believe and trust in Him. He lives within and among them through the Holy Spirit.

One thing we cannot obtain by being the best person we can be is our salvation. Jesus has accomplished this on the cross, where God's demand for uncompromising righteousness was matched by His love. A right standing with God is available by no other means. Jesus therefore said:

"I am the way and the truth and the life. No one comes to the Father except through Me."

Even if you do not yet believe in the God who presents Himself in the Person of Jesus Christ, consider how remarkable it is that one man, a handful of fisherman and a few other people could have so many followers. This man, who was the son of a woman, not even 15 years old when she carried Him, and who was only trained as a carpenter, divided history into BC and AD.

Glory to God, Who gives us victory through what His Son has done for us, and by His Spirit who dwells in those who believe and follow Him. Satan has been convicted of orchestrating the murder of an innocent Man on the cross. We are awaiting the execution of God's sentence on him and all his followers.

Disobedience is, more than any other factor, responsible for the problems of humankind on earth. Only acceptance of God's salvation plan by an act of faith and obedience can turn this around. www.wondernewbirth.com

God's salvation plan for the human race cannot be ignored, or regarded as unnecessary. He was prepared to let his Son die for it. What else can be more important?

"For God so loved the world that He gave His one and only Son, that whoever believes in Him shall not perish but have eternal life." This was the greatest gift He could give.

"I am the light of the world. Whoever follows Me will never walk in darkness, but will have the light of life."

The Bible teaches that there is no person on earth who ever lived, except Jesus Christ, who has never sinned. Therefore, no one can enter the unapproachable light of God's presence. The fellowship between God and Man was interrupted when Adam and Eve rebelled against God and caused the whole human race to be subject to Satan and sin.

"all have sinned and fall short of the glory of God."

The only way to reconcile God and Humankind was for Jesus Christ to die on the cross.

"But He was pierced for our transgressions, He was crushed for our iniquities; the punishment that brought us peace was on Him, and by His wounds we are healed. We all, like sheep, have gone astray, each of us has turned to our own way; and the Lord has laid on Him the iniquity of us all."

Jesus "asked His disciples, "'Who do people say the Son of Man is?' They replied, 'Some say John the Baptist; others say Elijah; and still others, Jeremiah or one of the prophets.' **'But what about you?' He asked. 'Who do you say I am?'** Simon Peter answered, 'You are the Christ, the Son of the living God.' Jesus replied, 'Blessed are you, Simon son of Jonah, for this was not revealed to you by man, but by my Father in heaven.'"

By saying the following words from your heart, you can become a citizen in the Kingdom of God and experience the transformation power of the cross and resurrection of Jesus:

"Jesus, I know I am a sinner, because I have rebelled against God, and I repent of this, and of every other sin in my life, as you will reveal to me now and in future. I realise that I cannot save myself, but I pray that you will save me. Thank you that there is no one too good or too bad for you to save. I believe that you died on the cross also for my sins and that God raised you from the dead, so that I can live with you. I declare before earth and heaven that you are Lord, Jesus, and I want to acknowledge you as my Lord. I want to follow wherever you lead me."

"If you declare with your mouth, 'Jesus is Lord' and believe in your heart that God raised Him from the dead, you will be saved."

You now have the assurance that Jesus has brought you out of eternal death to eternal life. Congratulations! A very significant change has happened in you; the Spirit of God has regenerated your spirit, which was "dead in sin", to become alive. You may or may not feel different immediately because this "newly born spirit" has to grow. It may grow at a variable pace, but if you follow the guidelines in the rest of this book, based on the bible, you will get stronger and stronger. Something so wonderful has happened to you, that God's angels in heaven are rejoicing.

"In the same way, I tell you, there is rejoicing in the presence of the angels of God over one sinner who repents."

And now, the following promise is for you as for every child of God.

"I am convinced that neither death nor life, neither angels nor demons, neither the present nor the future, nor any powers, neither height nor depth, nor anything else in all creation, will be able to separate us from the love of God that is in Christ Jesus our Lord."

By his grace, God gives us faith. Without faith, it is impossible to believe. When you have faith and believe, like going through an open door, you discover the reality of God's Kingdom. By praying the prayer as you did, you are "inside the room." The words of the bible and the spiritual truths will become clear to you now.

"Sanctify them by the truth; Your word is truth."

"Then you will know the truth, and the truth will set you free."

You may even say, "I didn't realise that my eyes have been so closed to what God wants to teach me!" But even so, there are many things you still have to learn and experience, and there will always be things you will only understand later.

"Now we see but a poor reflection as in a mirror; then we shall see face to face. Now I know in part; then I shall know fully, even as I am fully known."

"And after He had said these things, He was lifted up while they were looking on, and a cloud received Him out of their sight. And as they were gazing intently into the sky while He was going, behold, two men in white clothing stood beside them. They also said, "Men of Galilee, why do you stand looking into the sky? This Jesus, who has been taken up from you into heaven, will come in just the same way as you have watched Him go into heaven."

"For this reason also, God highly exalted Him, and bestowed on Him the name which is above every name, so that at the name of Jesus every knee will bow, of those who are in heaven and on earth and under the earth, and that every tongue will confess that Jesus Christ is Lord, to the glory of God the Father."

Growth

Our salvation is the result of what Christ has done for us on the cross, and nobody can boast.

"…because by the works of the law no one will be justified."

Everyone confronted with the gospel needs to make a choice to accept it or not. It is the foundation on which each person needs to build his or her life in the Kingdom.

"work out your salvation with fear and trembling; for it is God who is at work in you, both to will and to work for His good pleasure."

If you build the best you can with His power and his grace, you build with gold.

"If anyone builds on this foundation using gold, silver, costly stones, wood, hay or straw, their work will be shown for what it is, because the Day will bring it to light."

To be the best person you can be need not be a selfish ambition. We have been created by God for His glory. He wants us to use what He has given us to the best of our ability.

"It will be like a man going on a journey, who called his servants and entrusted to them his property. To one he gave five talents, to another two talents, to another one talent, to each according to his ability."

"But you, dear friends, by building yourselves up in your most holy faith and praying in the Holy Spirit, keep yourselves in God's love as you wait for the mercy of our Lord Jesus Christ to bring you to eternal life."

The following are nine important ways to strengthen your new life; you can start doing them all together.

1. Learn to know God as your Father by having a relationship with Him through your position in Jesus.

   "Now this is eternal life: that they know You, the only true God, and Jesus Christ, whom You have sent."

2. Read the Word of God, the Bible. Meditate on it, speak it and do it.

3. Pray – talk to God – whenever you can and also make time to pray.

4. Join up with other believers and get baptized.

5. Bring the gospel and your personal testimony to others.

    "But in your hearts revere Christ as Lord. Always be prepared to give an answer to everyone who asks you to give the reason for the hope that you have. But do this with gentleness and respect…"

6. Ask God for the filling and the power of the Holy Spirit, or ask someone to pray with you.

7. Depend on God for your needs "And my God will meet all your needs according to the riches of his glory in Christ Jesus."

8. Depend on the healing power of God "who forgives all your sins and heals all your diseases, He may heal us directly or bless

other means "Then Isaiah said, 'Prepare a poultice of figs.' They did so and applied it to the boil, and he recovered."

9. Care for others and do the good works of your calling.

"'For I was hungry, and you gave Me something to eat; I was thirsty, and you gave Me something to drink; I was a stranger, and you invited Me in; naked, and you clothed Me; I was sick, and you visited Me; I was in prison, and you came to Me... The King will reply 'Truly I tell you, whatever you did for one of the least of these brothers and sisters of mine, you did for Me.'"

"For we are God's handiwork, created in Christ Jesus to do good works, which God prepared in advance for us to do."

Start to walk in victory over sin. The blood of Jesus cleanses us from sin and releases us from the bondage of sin. Our 'default mode' should now be that we do not want to sin ('must not' has turned into 'want not') and though

Jesus has already paid for our past, present and future known and unknown sin on the cross, if we sin or do something wrong, we have to acknowledge it and repent. Apart from receiving forgiveness, this helps us not to do it again. We have to take responsibility for what we think, say and do. Jesus' blood was shed to take away our sin.

"If we claim to be without sin, we deceive ourselves and the truth is not in us. If we confess our sins, He is faithful and just and will forgive us our sins and purify us from all unrighteousness."

There are however real weaknesses, temptations and sickness which we should take to the cross. Giving in to these "weaknesses" which can be anything from an overt appetite for food, alcohol or sex, can lead to sin, and if given in to regularly leads to a bondage of sin which needs to be broken before it destroys us.

"When tempted, no one should say, 'God is tempting me.' For God cannot be tempted by evil, nor does He tempt anyone; but each person is tempted when they are dragged away by their own evil desire and enticed. Then, after desire has conceived, it gives birth to sin; and sin, when it is full-grown, gives birth to death."

To combat pride we can say with Paul: "May I never boast except in the cross of our Lord Jesus Christ, through which the world has been crucified to me, and I to the world."

Satan and his demons, will try to tell you that God is there to spoil your life. On the contrary, He is the giver of all the real joys we can experience on earth. Within the limits of His love for us and surrounded by His wisdom, we are free – our freedom only limited by the freedom of those around us. In this regard, we can experience:

The joy of knowing Him and worshipping Him in freedom. "But for you who fear My name, the sun of righteousness shall rise with healing in its wings. You shall go out leaping like calves from the stall."

The joy of seeking for His Kingdom to come. "...Your kingdom come, Your will be done, on earth as it is in heaven."

The joy of being able to be free from guilt. "Therefore, there is now no condemnation for those who are in Christ Jesus,"

The joy of friendship and love for one another. "I no longer call you servants, because a servant does not know his master's business. Instead, I have called you friends, for everything that I learned from my Father I have made known to you."

"By this everyone will know that you are My disciples, if you love one another."

The joy of love and sex. "May your fountain be blessed, and may you rejoice in the wife of your youth.

A loving doe, a graceful deer—
may her breasts satisfy you always,
may you ever be intoxicated with
her love."

The joy of children and being part of a
family. "Children are a heritage from
the Lord, offspring a reward from
Him."

"For this reason I kneel before the
Father, from whom every family in
heaven and on earth derives its
name."

The joy of food and wine. "Go, eat
your food with gladness, and drink
your wine with a joyful heart..."

The joy of looking at His creation. "When I consider Your heavens, the work of Your fingers, the moon and the stars, which You have set in place,"

"The earth is the Lord's, and everything in it, the world, and all who live in it"

The joy of fulfilment. "Delight yourself in the Lord, and He will give you the desires of your heart."

The joy of salvation and of eternal life. "I give them eternal life, and they shall never perish; no one will snatch them out of My hand."

The joy of being filled with His Spirit. "Do not get drunk on wine, which leads to debauchery. Instead, be filled with the Spirit, speaking to one another with psalms, hymns, and songs from the Spirit. Sing and make music from your heart to the Lord, always giving thanks to God the Father for everything, in the name of our Lord Jesus Christ."

"for the joy of the Lord is your strength."

"Finally, brothers and sisters, whatever is true, whatever is noble, whatever is right, whatever is pure, whatever is lovely, whatever is admirable – if anything is excellent or praiseworthy – think about such things."

One thing that will strengthen our faith more than any other is to be a witness for Him.

"I am not ashamed of the gospel, because it is the power of God that brings salvation to everyone who believes."

"He said to them, 'Go into all the world and preach the good news to all creation.'"

"Therefore go and make disciples of all nations, baptising them in the name of the Father and of the Son and of the Holy Spirit, and teaching them to obey everything I have commanded you. And surely I am with you always, to the very end of the age"

We should be prayerfully ready to seize every opportunity to do so. As we go along, we will look forward to the opportunities He gives us, rather than it being a burden. Witnessing is also a way for believers to connect with one another and build up their faith.

"Therefore, encourage one another and build each other up, just as in fact you are doing."

Remember what it is about for all of us: "the glorious riches of this mystery, which is Christ in you, the hope of glory."

We have the best help and back-up available.

When Jesus left the earth temporarily, He said that He would send us a Helper, to be with us and encourage us. This was, next to salvation, the greatest gift He could give to his church and individually to every child of Him.

"But the Comforter (Counsellor, Helper, Intercessor, Advocate, Strengthener, Standby), the Holy Spirit, Whom the Father will send in My name [in My place, to represent Me and act on My behalf], He will teach you all things. And He will cause you to recall (will remind you of, bring to your remembrance) everything I have told you."

He said, for us to be effective witnesses we need to be **empowered** by the Holy Spirit, who will also remind us of Jesus' words. He will also make Jesus and the Father real to us. He will bring love and unity among us so that everyone will know that we belong to Jesus, just as He did for the disciples in the beginning. He uses the blood of Jesus to clean us and to keep us clean. He fills our lives and brings the Joy of the Lord to our hearts.

"You have filled my heart with greater joy than when the grain and new wine abound." To be happy we don't need to be intoxicated by drugs or alcohol. "Do not get drunk on wine... Instead, be filled with the Spirit."

How do we receive the Holy Spirit? When we become Christians we are filled with the Holy Spirit, but we usually have to seek Him, or have someone pray over us, to receive his power. It is by the power of the Holy Spirit that the Church was established and He still enables his children to be his witnesses.

The armour God gives us to overcome the Enemy. (Read: Ephesians 6:13-18)

SALVATION (HELMET)
RIGHTEOUSNESS
(BREASTPLATE)
TRUTH (BELT)
FAITH (SHIELD)
WORD OF GOD (SWORD)
READINESS FOR THE
GOSPEL OF PEACE
(SHOES)

PRAY IN THE SPIRIT

Never forget that you have been 'born again' and now have the right to walk in the power of Christ.

"Therefore, if anyone is in Christ, they are a new creation; the old has gone, the new has come!"

Apart from the eradication of evil and the resurrection of the dead, the world and the known universe will be made new at the end of the present dispensation.

"Then I saw a new heaven and a new earth, for the first heaven and the first earth had passed away"

"He will wipe every tear from their eyes. There will be no more death' or mourning or crying or pain, for the old order of things has passed away."

"Then the angel showed me the river of the water of life, as clear as crystal, flowing from the throne of God and of the Lamb down the middle of the great street of the city. On each side of the river stood the tree of life, bearing twelve crops of fruit, yielding its fruit every month. And the leaves of the tree are for the healing of the nations. No longer will there be any curse. The throne of God and of the Lamb will be in the city, and His servants will serve Him. They will see His face, and His name will be on their foreheads. There will be no more night. They will not need the light of a lamp or the light of the sun, for the Lord God will give them light. And they will reign for ever and ever."

"The Spirit and the bride say, 'Come!' And let the one who hears say, 'Come!' Let the one who is thirsty come; and let the one who wishes take the free gift of the water of life."

"Come, Lord Jesus."

This table will tell you where in the
Bible you can find all the scriptures
quoted above (book chapter:verse).
They are all from the New Internati onal
Version (NIV) unless stated otherwise.
Why not look them up in context, and
try to memorise some of them?

Or use the table for a bible quiz?

Page15	There is no fear A new command	1 John 4:18 John 13:34
16	so we know these three remain Love the Lord Love is something	1 John 4:16 1 Corinth 13:13 Luke 10:27 Katherine Kuhlm
17	Not by might Do not suppose Remember	Zech 4:6 Matthew 10:34 John 15:20
18	I tell you a time is coming	Luke 12:4 John 16:2
19	You have heard Do not take For our struggle is	Matthew 5:43 Romans 12:19 Ephesians 6:12
20	God is light	1 John 1:5

P 21	The one who	Revelation 3:5
	That all of them	John 17:21
	Christ in you	Colossians 1:27
22	But God	Romans 5:8
	This is good	1 Timothy 2:3
23	Whoever comes	John 6:37
	Without faith	Hebrews 11:6
24	Our Father	Matthew 6:9
26	The Spirit of God	Genesis 1:2
27	As He was praying	Luke 3:21
	Therefore go	Matthew 28:19
28	Let anyone	John 7:37
	My food	John 4:34
	Jesus answered	Matthew 4:4
29	How you have fallen	Isaiah 14:12
33	In the beginning	John 1:1
34	So God created	Genesis 1:27
36	What good is it	Mark 8:36

P 37	God is Spirit For with You	John 4:24 Psalm 36:9
39	Be self-controlled	1 Peter 5:8
31	And no wonder The devil	2 Corinth' 11:14 John 8:44
41	In the sixth month	Luke 1:26
42	Therefore the Lord For a child will be	Isaiah 7:14 Isaiah 9:6
44	I am the Way	John 14:6
46	For God so loved	John 3:16
47	I am the light	John 8:12
48	All have sinnedBut He was pierced	Romans 3:23 Isaiah 53:5
49	asked His disciples	Matt16:13-17
51	If you declare	Romans 10:9
52	In the same way	Luke 15:10

P 53	I am convinced	Romans 8:38
54	Sanctify them Then you will know	John 17:17 John 8:32
55	Now we see He was take up	1 Corinth' 13:12 Acts 1:9-11
56	God highly exalted	Phil 2:9-11
57	Because by the Work out your	Galatians 2:16 Philippians 2:12
58	If anyone builds	1 Corinth' 3:12
59	It will be like a man But you dear friend	Matthew 25:14 Jude 1:20
60	Now this is eternal	John 17:3
61	But in your hearts	1 Peter 3:15
62	Meets needs Heals diseases	Phil 4:19 Ps 103:3
63	Bless other means For I was hungry	2 Kings 20:7 Matthew 25:35

P 64	For we are God's	Eph 2:10
65	If we claim	1 John 1:8
66	When tempted	James 1:13
67	May I never boast	Galatians 6:14
68	But for you who revere My name Your kingdom Therefore there is	Malachi 4:2 Matthew 6:10 Romans 8:1
69	I no longer call By this everyone May your fountain	John 15:15 John 13:35 Proverbs 5:18
70	Children are a heritage For this reason Go eat your food	Psalm 127:3 Ephesians 3:14 Ecclesiastes 9:7
71	When I consider The earth is Delight yourself I give them eternal	Psalm 8:3 Psalm 24:1 Psalm 37:4 John 10:28

P 72	Be filled with the	Ephesians 5:18
	For the joy	Nehemiah 8:10
73	Finally brothers and sisters	Philippians 4:8
	I am not ashamed	Romans 1:16
74	He said to them	Mark 16:15
	Therefore go	Matthew 28:19
75	Therefore encourage	1 Thess 5:11
	The glorious riches	Colossians 1:27
76	But the Comforter	John 14:26 (Amplified Bible)
78	You have filled	Psalm 4:7
	Do not get drunk	Ephesians 5:18
79	Salvation	Ephesians 6:13
80	Therefore if anyone	2 Corinth' 5:17
	Then I saw	Revelation 21:1
81	He will wipe	Revelation 21:4
	Then the angel	Revelation 22:1
82	The Spirit and the bride	Revelation 22:17
	Come Lord Jesus	Revelation 22:20

Citizenship

To become a citizen of any country, you have to comply with the rules of that country for naturalisation. You cannot change their rules to suit yourself.

The same applies for naturalisation to the Kingdom of God. The rules that I have written about in this book are based on the Bible: they are final and cannot be changed.

Your eternal destiny is at stake! You cannot reach the Kingdom of God by your own efforts or by living a good life – any more than a good swimmer can cross the Atlantic Ocean without a plane or a ship.

For guidance see pages 50-51

In my personal testimony, I described how I believe God called me many years ago to become a follower of His Son and how I responded to it.

If you sense that He is calling you now, please do not ignore His call, but accept His salvation plan. Do not wait until later to discover that what is written in this book is the truth, but later had become too late to do something about it.

My sincere prayer is that this book may help you to start with, or experience, a closer walk with God, and that it will encourage you to want to know Him better.

If you want to get or share information, or need a copy in large print: e mail me at: bestcanbe@googlemail.com
Marius

Editing by Diane Morrison

www.justabook.co.uk

Jesus Christ did what no other could do. He spoke about Himself as no other can speak, and when He comes back, He will be greater than anybody can imagine

There is *nothing* more important in this life and for eternity than to have our broken relationship with God restored